Folk Songs for Solo Singers, *Vol. 2*

14 Folk Songs Arranged for Solo Voice and Piano... For Recitals, Concerts and Contests

COMPILED AND EDITED BY JAY ALTHOUSE

Contents

Cover art: *After the Dry Spell* c. 1975
by Mattie Lou O'Kelley (American, b. 1908)
Acrylic on canvas (24" x 32 1/4")
Collection of the Museum of American Folk Art, New York;
Gift of Mr. and Mrs. Edwin C. Braman, 1983.14.1

ABOUT THE COVER

Mattie Lou O'Kelley, a native of rural Georgia, began painting at the age of 60. Her memory paintings, often idyllic landscapes or farm scenes filled with people and animals, depict her early life in Georgia. Ms. O'Kelley's early paintings were displayed in the museum shop at the High Museum of Art in Atlanta where they were discovered by Robert Bishop, director of the American Museum of Folk Art. Her works are now included in the collections of major museums.

Several of the solos in this collection are also available as choral arrangements from Alfred Publishing Co., Inc.

Folk Songs for Solo Singers, Volume 2 is the fifth in the " *...for Solo Singers*" series. If you enjoyed this collection you should look at *Folk Songs for Solo Singers, Spirituals for Solo Singers, Favorite Sacred Classics for Solo Singers*, and *Christmas for Solo Singers*. For further information, see the back cover.

Glossary of Nautical terms used in "Fire Down Below"

Boom:	Poles (or spars) projecting from a mast.
Bunk :	Sleeping quarters.
Dodger:	The sheltering canvas cover for a hatch.
Fo'c's'l:	(fore castle) The deck in front of the fore mast.
Galley:	The kitchen or cooking area.
Head:	The lavatory.
Hook:	The anchor.
Jenny:	A large forward sail.
Lazarette:	A storage locker, usually in the stern.
Locker:	The place where personal belongings are stored.
Mains'l:	(mainsail) The principal sail on the main mast.
Mizzen:	(mizzenmast) The third mast from forward in a ship with three or more masts.
Pulpit:	A safety rail extending around the bow or stern.
Rigging:	Ropes used to support and work the masts and sails.
Shoal:	A sandbank or sand bar in shallow water.
Sole:	The floor of the cabin interior.
Stays'l:	(staysail) A triangular sail fastened on a stay (a supporting wire for the mast).
Tiller:	A bar or lever used to turn the rudder.
Yard:	A spar fastened at right angles across a mast and used to support a sail.

THE WATER IS WIDE

American Folk Song
Arranged by MARK HAYES

CINDY

American Folk Song
Arranged by JAY ALTHOUSE

ought to see my Cin - dy, she lives a - way down South. And
wish I was a rich man with cash in sev - 'ral banks. I

she's so sweet the hon - ey bees swarm a - round her mouth. Get a - long
sure would buy nice things for her to hear her whis - per, "Thanks."

I

It's

Cin - dy in the spring-time, and Cin - dy in the fall. If

I can't have my Cin - dy, I'll have no girl at all. Get a-long

12

ALL THROUGH THE NIGHT

Welsh Carol
Arranged by RUTH ELAINE SCHRAM

Gently, with feeling (♩ = 70)

Sleep, my child, and peace at-tend thee, All through the night. Guard-ian an-gels God will send thee, All through the night. Soft the drow-sy hours are creep-ing,

POOR BOY

American Folk Song
Arranged by RUTH ELAINE SCHRAM

Tenderly, in one (♩ = ca. 132)

As I went down to the riv - er, poor boy, to see the ships go by, _____ my sweet - heart stood on the deck of

one, where she waved to me good-bye. _____ Bow

8vb

down your head and cry, poor boy, bow down your *mf*

head and cry; _____ and stop think-ing of the

poco rall. *a tempo*

one you love, bow down your head and cry. _____

poco rall. *a tempo*

19

cry; _____ and stop think - ing of the one you

love, bow down your head and cry. _____ Bow

down your head, and cry; _____

cry. _____

CAMPTOWN RACES

Arranged by
JAY ALTHOUSE

Words and Music by
STEPHEN FOSTER

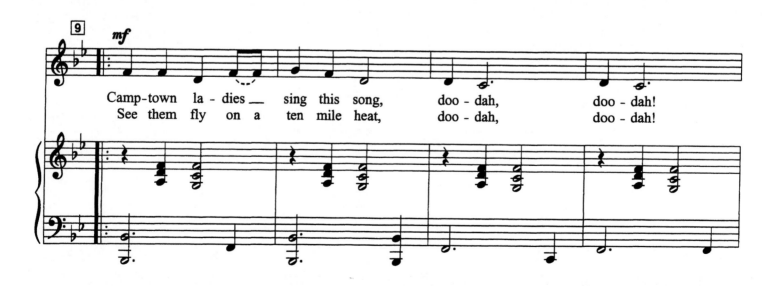

Camp-town la - dies___ sing this song, doo - dah, doo - dah!
See them fly on a ten mile heat, doo - dah, doo - dah!

24

GO 'WAY FROM MY WINDOW

American Folk Song
Arranged by RUTH ELAINE SCHRAM

28

SIMPLE GIFTS

Shaker Tune
Arranged by MARK HAYES

'Tis the gift to be sim-ple, 'Tis the

gift to be free, 'Tis the gift to come down where we ought to be, And

when we find our-selves in the place just right, ____ 'Twill

be in the val - ley of love _____ and de -

light. _____ 'Tis the

gift to be sim-ple, 'Tis the gift to be free, 'Tis the gift to come down

where we ought to be, And when we find our-selves in the place just right, 'Twill

Slower, freely (♩ = 84)

When true sim - plic - i - ty is gained, To bow and to bend we

shan't be a-shamed, To turn, turn will be our de-light, Till by

turn - ing, turn - ing we come _____ 'round

right. _____

Faster (♩ = 96)

8vb

POOR WAYFARING STRANGER

American Folk Ballad
Arranged by JAY ALTHOUSE

35

HE'S GONE AWAY

American Folk Song
Arranged by RUTH ELAINE SCHRAM

He's gone a-way _____ for to stay a lit-tle

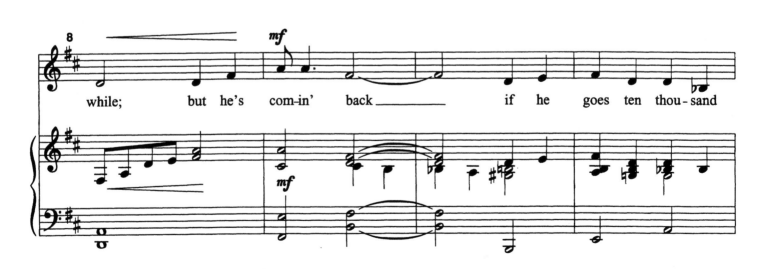

while; but he's com-in' back _____ if he goes ten thou-sand

* Yandro: a mountain in North Carolina.

* Bring out melody in piano.

OLD DAN TUCKER

American Folk Song
Arranged by JAY ALTHOUSE

Old Dan Tuck-er. You're too late to get your sup-per. Sup-per's o - ver and

din-ner's cook-in', and Old Dan Tuck-er stands there look-in'.

Old Dan Tuck-er is a nice old man. He used to ride our Der-by ram. He

rode that ram right down the hill. _ If he had-n't got up, he'd be there still.

ALL MY TRIALS

American Folk Song
Arranged by RUTH ELAINE SCHRAM

FOLLOW THE DRINKING GOURD

Additional new words
by JAY ALTHOUSE

Traditional
Arranged by JAY ALTHOUSE

Note: The "drinking gourd" refers to The Big Dipper which pointed the way north for slaves escaping to freedom prior to and during the American Civil War.

FIRE DOWN BELOW

Verse 1: Traditional
Other verses by JAY ALTHOUSE
and CAP'N. DOUG TAYLOR

Sea Chantey
Arranged by JAY ALTHOUSE

For a glossary of the nautical terms used in this song, see page 2.

58

that's not what I dread. The

on - ly fire___ that I fear _____ is

fire in the head. Yo ho! Yo ho! There's

fire down be - low. So fetch a buck - et of wa - ter, boys, there's

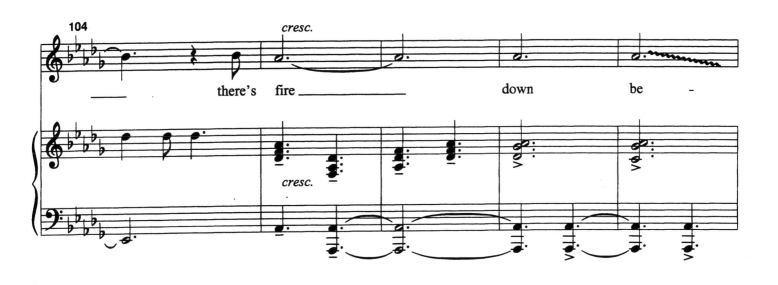

SHENANDOAH

American Folk Song
Arranged by JAY ALTHOUSE

64

8vb